FUN FACTS

Ripley's Believe It or Not!®

Kids

& SILLY STORIES

ODD
AROUND THE
WORLD!

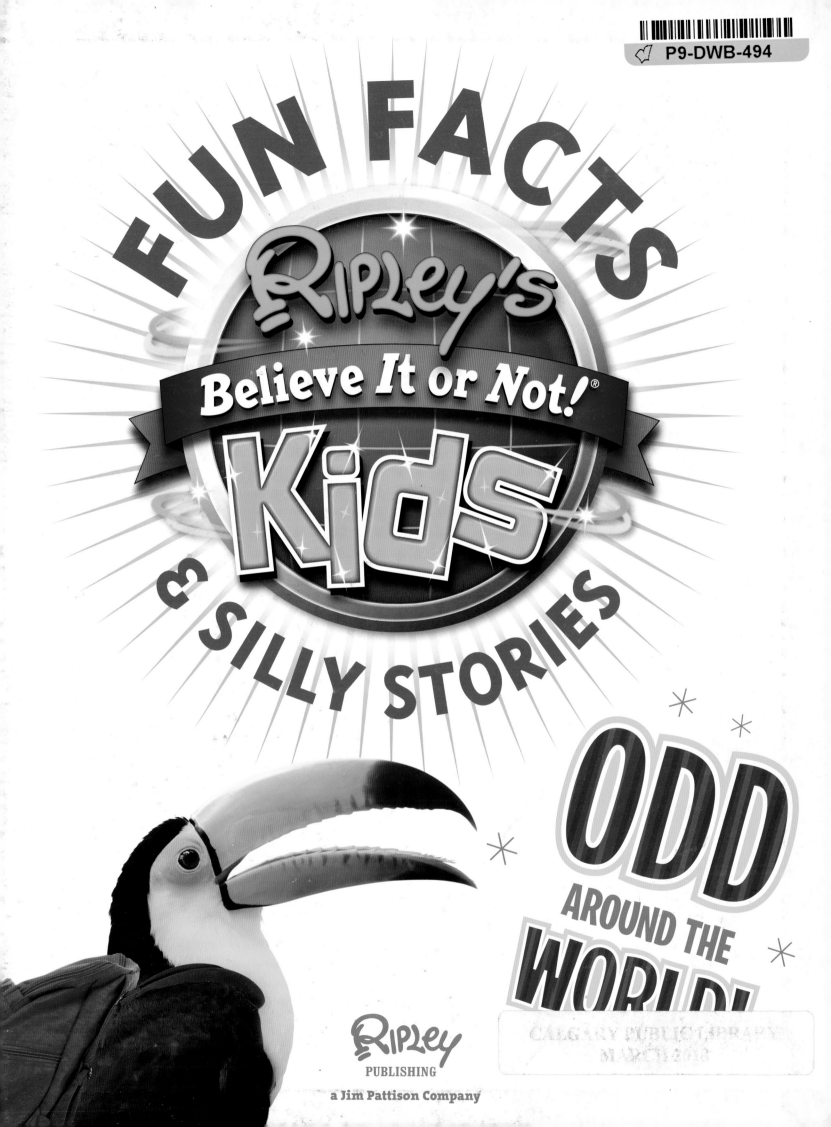

RIPLEY
PUBLISHING

a Jim Pattison Company

What's Inside?

Games & Puzzles Galore!

Silly Stories!

Terrific Travels!

A Tasty Recipe!

Page 90

Page 122

Fantastic Festivals!

Unbelievable Facts!

Page 76

Page 104

Check THIS Out

REALLY?
Giant moose sculpture

NO WAY!
Dog-shaped hotel

CUTE
Road for ducks

CRAZY
Flip-flop creations

WOW!
Pink sand beaches

Plan Your Trip

The inside of the Ninja New York restaurant looks like a Japanese feudal village—and ninja waiters sneak up on diners at any time!

I have mad ninja skills. Don't make me use them!

If you have a fun fact or a silly story, email it to us at bionresearch@ripleys.com

FUN FACTS

Ripley's Believe It or Not!® Kids

& SILLY STORIES

5

Check out these books for more Fun Facts & Silly Stories!

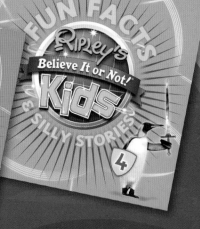

ACKNOWLEDGMENTS

Front Cover © Maciej Czekajewski-Shutterstock.com, © Africa Studio-Shutterstock.com; **Back Cover** (tr) © Michael Kraus-Shutterstock.com, (bl) Annabella Charles Photography; **IFC** © Daniel Leppens-Shutterstock.com; **2** (t) Instagram.com/sweetiecapy, (b) © Andrey Yurlov-Shutterstock.com; **2-3** (t) © Rob Hainer-Shutterstock.com, (b) © aphotostory-Shutterstock.com; **3** (t) © Jag_cz-Shutterstock.com, (b) © ilikestudio-Shutterstock.com; **4** © rudall30-Masterfile.com; **5** (tc) © Nico Traut-Shutterstock.com, (tr) © Chris Ison-Shutterstock.com, © Alexander Ryabintsev-Shutterstock.com, (br) © FotoYakov-Shutterstock.com; **6** (t) © Alex Oakenman-Shutterstock.com, (b) SunglassCat; **7** (t) ChinaFotoPress/ChinaFotoPress via Getty Images, (c) Brighton Argus/Solent News/REX Shutterstock, (b) Ian Berry. www.ian-berry.com; **8** (cl) © Samuel Borges Photography-Shutterstock.com, (cl) © Npeter-Shutterstock.com, (b) © Robyn Mackenzie-Shutterstock.com; **9** © Samuel Borges Photography-Shutterstock.com; **10-11** © Stuart Pearce / Alamy Stock Photo; **11** © M L Pearson / Alamy Stock Photo; **12-13** Boaz Rottem; **14** (tl) © Cuson-Shutterstock.com, (tl) © Ivonne Wierink-Shutterstock.com, (tr) © bluedog studio-Shutterstock.com; **15** (tl) © JDCarballo-Shutterstock.com, (tr) © Eric Isselee-Shutterstock.com, (bc) © Fly_dragonfly-Shutterstock.com, (br) © Birgit Reitz-Hofmann-Shutterstock.com; **16** IAIN WATTS/MERCURY PRESS; **17** © photoplotnikov-Shutterstock.com, (bkg) IAIN WATTS/MERCURY PRESS; **18** © R. MACKAY PHOTOGRAPHY, LLC-Shutterstock.com, © Ugorenkov Aleksandr-Shutterstock.com, © sergign-Shutterstock.com, © Nordling-Shutterstock.com, © Yurii Vydyborets-Shutterstock.com, © Luis Carlos Torres-Shutterstock.com, © SviP-Shutterstock.com, © Richard Peterson-Shutterstock.com, © mtkang-Shutterstock.com, © Javier Brosch-Shutterstock.com, © Elnur-Shutterstock.com, © Maglara-Shutterstock.com, © Javier Brosch-Shutterstock.com; **20** © cynoclub-Masterfile.com; **20-21** © Spumador-Shutterstock.com; **21** Peter Charlesworth/LightRocket via Getty Images; **22** © ifong-Shutterstock.com, © Susan Schmitz-Shutterstock.com; **23** (tl) © ilikestudio-Shutterstock.com, (c) © PhotoNAN-Shutterstock.com, (br) © Africa Studio-Shutterstock.com; **24** (t) © chrisbrignell-Shutterstock.com, (b) © Minerva Studio-Shutterstock.com; **25** (t) © Deklofenak-Masterfile.com, (c) © Javier Brosch-Shutterstock.com, (b) © Milkovasa-Shutterstock.com; **26** @DAXON / CATERS NEWS; **27** @DAXON / CATERS NEWS; **28-29** Vj Suave - Ygor Marotta; **31** © MANDY GODBEHEAR-Shutterstock.com; **32** © Nicescene-Shutterstock.com; **33** (t) ChinaFotoPress/ChinaFotoPress via Getty Images, (c) © Eric Isselee-Shutterstock.com, (b) © Gustavo Frazao-Shutterstock.com; **34-35** © Henry Westheim Photography / Alamy Stock Photo; **35** (tr ,cr, br) © Daniel Leppens-Shutterstock.com; **36** (cl) © yyang-Shutterstock.com, (b) © Tribune Content Agency LLC / Alamy Stock Photo; **37** (t) The Asahi Shimbun via Getty Images, (b) © jgorzynik-Shutterstock.com; **38-39** Annabella Charles Photography; **40** © Naghiyev-Shutterstock.com; **40-41** Taxi Fabric; **42** (tr) © Africa Studio-Shutterstock.com; **43** (tr) © Naghiyev-Shutterstock.com, (bl) © smej-Shutterstock.com, (bc) © saiko3p-Shutterstock.com, (bc) © Mario Savoia-Shutterstock.com, (br) © Pikoso.kz-Shutterstock.com; **44** (cl) © Rob Cousins / Alamy Stock Photo, (br) © Michael Jenner / Alamy Stock Photo; **45** (tr) © Franck Fotos / Alamy Stock Photo, (bl) © roy henderson-Shutterstock.com; **46** Bethany Clarke/Getty Images for Canal & River Trust; **47** (l) ASSOCIATED PRESS, (r) Kyodo via AP Images; **48** © javarman-Shutterstock.com; **49** (sp) © Vadim Georgiev-Shutterstock.com, (tl) © Gerisima-Shutterstock.com, (r) © Sergey Novikov-Shutterstock.com; **50** (t) TOBIAS SCHWARZ/AFP/Getty Images, (b) © genlock-Shutterstock.com; **50-51** (dps) © Stephanie Zieber-Shutterstock.com; **51** (t) © Bornfree-Shutterstock.com, (b) © s_bukley-Shutterstock.com; **52** (t) © Pakhnyushchy-Shutterstock.com, (b) Courtesy of NASA; **53** (t) Courtesy of NASA; **54-55** (t, b) Photos courtesy Sheyna E. Gifford, livefrommars.life; **55** (tr) Photo courtesy of Carmel Johnston; **56** Courtesy of James Holmdahl; **56-57** (sp) © kevron2001-Masterfile.com; **57** U-PET by L&T International Group Inc.; **58** (bl) © Jurgen Freund/naturepl.com; **58-59** (dps) © Ammit Jack-Shutterstock.com; **59** (c) © Jeff Grabert-Shutterstock.com; **60** (sp) © Angel DiBilio-Shutterstock.com; **61** (tl) © Tarbell Studio Photo-Shutterstock.com, (bl, br) © Laboko-Shutterstock.com; **62** © Igor Sokolov (breeze)-Shutterstock.com; **63** (t) © Alexander Ryabintsev-Shutterstock.com, (b) Photo courtesy of Alextelford at en.wikipedia (CC BY-SA 3.0): http://creativecommons.org/licenses/by-sa/3.0/; **64-65** Images courtesy of Ocean Sole, http://www.ocean-sole.com; **66-67** CATERS NEWS; **68-69** DAN ROWLANDS / CATERS NEWS; **70** Adare Manor; **71** (sp) Adare Manor, (b) © cammep-Shutterstock.com; **72** (b) Kakslauttanen Arctic Resort. www.kakslauttanen.fi. Photographer Valtteri Hirvonen; **72-73** © Atiketta Sangasaeng-Shutterstock.com; **73** (b) Kakslauttanen Arctic Resort. www.kakslauttanen.fi; **74-75** © Volt Collection-Shutterstock.com; **75** (tl) © Mega Pixel-Shutterstock.com, (tr) © Zoltan Major-Shutterstock.com, (b) © Mega Pixel-Shutterstock.com; **76** © aphotostory-Shutterstock.com; **77** © aphotostory-Shutterstock.com; **78** © Kotomiti Okuma-Shutterstock.com; **79** © Shchipkova Elena-Shutterstock.com; **80** (t) © MAHATHIR MOHD YASIN-Shutterstock.com, © Fablok-Shutterstock.com, (c) © Andrey Lobachev-Shutterstock.com, (b) © Designsstock-Shutterstock.com; **81** (t) © Maxi_m-Shutterstock.com, (c) © robtek-Shutterstock.com, (b) © Richard Peterson-Shutterstock.com; **82-83** Instagram.com/sweetiecapy; **84** (b) © murphy81-Shutterstock.com; **84-85** © allx-Masterfile.com; **85** (tr) © pirke-Shutterstock.com, (bl) © Ignatius Sariputra-Shutterstock.com; **86** IAN MUNRO / CATERS NEWS; **87** (cr) © isselee-Masterfile.com, (b) ASSOCIATED PRESS; **88** Photo Credits: Dianne de Las Casas; **89** (tr) © Valentyn Volkov-Shutterstock.com, (bl) © Subbotina Anna-Shutterstock.com; **90** Photo Credits: Dianne de Las Casas; **90-91** © Jag_cz-Shutterstock.com; **92** © Susan Schmitz-Shutterstock.com; **92-93** © andrey_kuzmin-Masterfile.com; **93** © rprongjai-Shutterstock.com; **94-95** DC Comics Super Heroes Café (Marina Bay Sands, Singapore); **96** (b) © strfox-Masterfile.com; **96-97** (c) © Jose Ignacio Soto-Shutterstock.com, (b) © jamdesign-Masterfile.com; **97** (tr) © Andrey Yurlov-Shutterstock.com, (br) © UbjsP-Shutterstock.com; **99** (t) © robertosch-Masterfile.com, (b) © magann-Masterfile.com; **100-101** STR/AFP/Getty Images; **102** (t) Fairfax Media via Getty Images, (b) Max Mumby/Indigo/Getty Images; **103** kohlermedia.ch; **104** (b) © ilikestudio-Shutterstock.com; **104-105** SkyHighStudios/Getty Images; **105** (b) © Abel Tumik-Shutterstock.com, (b) © somyot pattana-Shutterstock.com; **106-107** The red blocks (two outermost images / red highlight) Photography: jerrymetellus.com, The central image (purple highlight) Photography: Zach Mahone; **108** © Alena Ozerova-Shutterstock.com; **109** © pbombaert-Shutterstock.com; **110** © AlekseyKarpenko-Shutterstock.com; **111** (t) © Manon van Os-Shutterstock.com, (b) AUSTIN CHERUPUZHA / CATERS NEWS; **112** The Asahi Shimbun via Getty Images; **113** (r) The Asahi Shimbun via Getty Images, (bl) Keith Tsuji/Getty Images; **114** (t) Photo courtesy of Jon Callas (CC BY 2.0), (b) © Alen Ferina / Alamy Stock Photo; **115** TONU TUNNEL / CATERS NEWS; **116-117** AJAY VERMA / CATERS NEWS AGENCY; **118-119** Photos courtesy of Laura Jackson; **120-121** Henryk T. Kaiser/REX/Shutterstock; **122** (cr) © Rob Hainer-Shutterstock.com, (br) © isselee-Masterfile.com; **122-123** (t) © FiledIMAGE-Shutterstock.com; **123** (tr) © isselee-Masterfile.com; **126** (b) Cem Oksuz/Anadolu Agency/Getty Images; **126-127** (dps) © michelangeloop-Shutterstock.com; **127** (t) © GTS Productions-Shutterstock.com; **128** (b) © Michael Kraus-Shutterstock.com; **128-129** (bkg) Roland Seitre/Minden Pictures; **129** (b) LYNN CAMPBELL / CATERS NEWS; **131** (tl) © Jagodka-Shutterstock.com, (br) © norikko-Shutterstock.com; **132-133** © Daniel Prudek-Shutterstock.com; **133** (b) © Gavin Maxwell/naturepl.com; **134** © MSSA-Shutterstock.com; © lyricsaima-Shutterstock.com; **134-135** © Suriya Sising-Shutterstock.com, © Filip Bjorkman-Shutterstock.com; **135** © lyricsaima-Shutterstock.com; **MASTER GRAPHICS** © Maciej Czekajewski-Shutterstock.com

Key: t = top, b = bottom, c = center, l = left, r = right, sp = single page, bkg = background

All other photos are from Ripley Entertainment Inc.

Every attempt has been made to acknowledge correctly and contact copyright holders, and we apologize in advance for any unintentional errors or omissions, which will be corrected in future editions.

When the mummy of Ramses II was sent to France in 1976, it was issued a passport!

VISAS

VISAS

EGYPT

ARRIVAL
Aéroport
PARIS
17.06.2012
REPUBLIQUE FRANCAISE

In the 1870s, a Belgian village tried to train 37 cats to deliver mail. (It didn't work.)

Don't Forget to Pack

YOUR PASSPORT!

German citizens are allowed to stick out their tongues in their passport photos!

A LUGGAGE LOCK!

Alan Freed collected over 11,000 lost or broken luggage locks while working at a Washington, DC, airport, later using them to create a giant padlock weighing over 300 lbs.!

SUNGLASSES!

Bagel the cat, born without eyelids, wears glasses to protect her eyes!

MONEY!

He Peiqi of Chongqing City, China, built a replica of his hometown using over 50,000 coins! He didn't use a drop of glue!

JEANS!

No one loves denim more than British artist Ian Berry, better known as Denimu. He carefully cuts, stitches, arranges, and pastes the panels into awesome urban landscapes.

A SWEATER!

An animal sanctuary in England knits woolly winter sweaters for its chickens! Hundreds of bald birds are now warm through the colder months thanks to the "chi-kinis."

Worldwide Whirly Word

Can you find all 15 cities hidden in this puzzle? Make sure to look up, down, backward, across, and diagonally!

ATHENS
BEIJING
MADRID
CAIRO
PARIS
BERLIN
JEDDAH
NAIROBI
NEW YORK
TOKYO
ROME
LONDON
TUNIS
LIMA
TORONTO

P	J	R	F	Q	L	Z	B	L	Q	U	F	G	I	A
J	E	D	D	A	H	O	I	Z	A	E	K	J	H	I
E	L	D	T	M	G	M	N	W	M	U	W	K	S	L
A	C	U	M	H	A	N	O	D	G	M	O	T	I	X
S	Q	E	A	L	W	E	X	F	O	R	U	B	O	A
T	Z	U	D	W	S	W	S	A	I	N	O	E	H	N
J	U	M	R	K	N	Y	P	A	Q	R	K	I	I	B
T	T	Q	I	D	B	O	C	G	I	N	N	J	D	R
F	O	X	D	E	Z	R	L	A	A	H	W	I	R	O
M	T	K	R	T	N	K	N	E	D	T	Q	N	E	R
L	G	L	Y	S	F	T	T	Z	B	V	H	G	V	K
Q	I	P	P	O	D	K	U	P	W	U	I	E	N	P
N	E	M	O	R	M	W	N	F	K	J	J	Q	N	Z
T	O	R	O	N	T	O	I	P	D	B	P	I	P	S
P	A	R	I	S	A	C	S	X	A	B	A	F	A	D

Want to check your answers? Turn to page 136 for the puzzle solution!

At Hotel Costa Verde, in Costa Rica's Manuel Antonio National Park, guests can stay in a 1965 Boeing 727 airplane that juts 50 feet into the jungle's canopy!

Weird Hotels

Located at the foot of China's Emei Mountain, the Haoduo Panda Hotel is unbearably cute, from the panda-themed rooms to the employees' uniforms—giant panda suits!

Hoisted 150 feet above Harlingen Harbor in The Netherlands, guests at the Crane Hotel can rotate their room 360 degrees!

The two-story-tall Dog Bark Park Inn in Cottonwood, Idaho, is built in the shape of a beagle! Pets are welcome, too!

TAIJI

Tea is always served with a twist at the Taiji Tea Ceremony House in Hangzhou, China. A Chinese acrobat will perform an ancient tai chi tea ceremony where he will bend over backward to prepare your tea, and then pour it into your cup—upside down!

TEA HOUSE

12

These orchids sure smell nice.

They smell better than that man's underwear!

Strange

Thai customs officials stopped a man with four birds and 50 rare orchids in his suitcase—and a pair of baby pygmy monkeys that he had inside his underwear!

A woman once tried to bring 75 live snakes in her bra—and six lizards in her shorts—onto an airplane in Sweden.

Smuggling

A woman from Thailand once tried to smuggle a sleeping baby tiger onto an airplane by hiding it in a suitcase with stuffed toys.

ZZZ

Up Pup and Away!

Woody, Helena, Holly, and Oban are four special guide dogs in England that help their partially sighted owners maneuver through airports and travel on planes. After their training, the dogs "graduated" by taking their first flight!

Afraid of flying? Therapy dogs at Charlotte Douglas International Airport in North Carolina help tense travelers relax with inviting "Pet Me" signs.

Milo, a six-year-old terrier from Cardiff, Wales, acts as a guide dog for his older brother, Eddie, a blind Labrador retriever.

Animal ROUND-UP

Can you find all ten differences between the suitcases? Have fun packing for your pet!

Are we there YET?

BONUS:
Spot the teeny tiny poisonous frog in the picture below.

Can you find the six differences between the two scenes? Color in the differences.

Every October on the feast day of the Patron Saint of Animals, Saint Francis of Assisi, pets all over the world are blessed by priests!

Want to check your answers?
Turn to page 136 for the puzzle solutions!

Rare Runways

Barra, Scotland, is home to the world's only scheduled beach-landing airport. Flights are dictated by the tide!

Singapore's Changi Airport boasts a butterfly garden with over 1,000 butterflies!

G-BZFP

fly

There is an 18-hole golf course sandwiched between the runways at Thailand's Don Muang International Airport!

A-MAZE-ING Airlines!

Use your pencil to help this frequent flyer find her lost luggage!

Want to check your answers? Turn to pages 136 for the puzzle solution!

START

END

Winging It

Get ready for takeoff! Here's ten first-class facts about airplanes!

The longest flight in the world is about 8,500 miles from Sydney, Australia, to Dallas, Texas—around 17 hours!

There are 5,000 airplanes in the sky above the United States at any given time!

Flying through a thunderstorm can expose airplane passengers to radiation levels equivalent to 400 chest X-rays!

Bar Nunn, Wyoming, was built on top of an abandoned airport in 1982. The old runways now serve as streets!

English is the international language of flight. All flight staff are required to speak English.

The runway at Gisborne Airport in New Zealand has operating train tracks running straight through it!

The Boeing® airplane plant in Washington State is so huge that Disneyland® could fit inside!

A plane going from Australia to Malaysia made an emergency landing when the 2,186 sheep in the cargo bay passed too much gas.

About 1 in 5 people have some fear of flying, or "aviophobia."

The world's shortest commercial flight—between the Westray and Papa Westray Orkney Islands—can be completed in just 47 seconds!

Selfie Sidekicks

Allan Dixon from Ireland is a real-life Dr. Dolittle—he's been able to "talk" over 30 different animal species from around the world into posing for a selfie!

VJ Suave

Brazilian artists Ceci Soloaga and Ygor Marotta, known as VJ Suave, created "suaveciclos"— tricycles with video projectors and speakers— to bring their vibrant animations to life against buildings, trees, and sidewalks all over the world!

We asked VJ Suave how they came up with their unique, on-the-go animation.

....

Q: What was the inspiration for using tricycles for the "suaveciclos"?

A: We needed two front wheels in order to carry our equipment in the front box. So, we decided to create an "audiovisual tricycle."

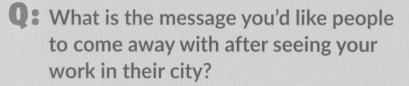

Q: What is the message you'd like people to come away with after seeing your work in their city?

A: We create our animations to communicate love, kindness, and to pass a positive message—and hope people will be surprised by our characters flying around their cities.

Your Odd Adventure

How many smaller words can you make out of the letters in the word below? Words must have four letters or more.

Want to check your answers? Turn to pages 137 for the puzzle solution!

ADVENTURE

Ask a friend to give you words...

...to fill in the blanks in this story...

...but don't let them peek!

On the _____ trip to _____ , my _____ friend
       adjective   **place**   **adjective**

and I decided to play a game. It was a very _____ trip, so we
                                           adjective

wanted to play a game with _____ and _____. Using
                            plural noun   **plural noun**

our_____ to _____ , we tried to get the_____
     noun   **verb**   **plural noun**

next to us to play along, but they just _____at us and
                                action verb

_____ away. After a few rounds, we thought the game could
  action verb

use some _____ so we turned on the _____ and
          plural noun   **noun**

started _____ to the _____ that came on. This
        action verb   **noun**

lasted for _____ before I got _____ and
     measurement of time   **adjective**

decided to_____. When we got hungry, we_____
     action verb   **action verb**

our_____ and ate _____ with _____for
    noun   **noun**   **noun**

dessert. We will never_____ that trip. It was the_____
                  verb   **adjective**

trip of my_____!
     noun

Now, read it out loud!

Travel Tidbits

In Scotland, the hesitation when you can't remember someone's name is called a "tartle."

A town in the Netherlands has a neighborhood where every street name is inspired by *The Lord of the Rings* trilogy, with roads paying tribute to hobbits, elves, and dwarves.

The turtle-shaped island of the Muodaoxi River in China appears once a year! Every spring, the river's low water level reveals the turtle shape of the island.

In the Torres Strait off the coast of Australia, you can visit Tuesday Island, Wednesday Island, Thursday Island, and Friday Island!

WEDNESDAY

FRIDAY

THURSDAY

TUESDAY

Weird Festivals

Shhh...

Ocean City, New Jersey, holds a "Quiet Festival" every November, where attractions include kite-flying and sign language.

Each year, Toyohashi, Japan, hosts an extreme fire festival! People set off huge homemade bamboo fireworks that explode just inches from their faces.

On the first Sunday of every September, the Bloemencorso, or flower parade, makes its way through the streets of the Dutch town of Zundert.

Train Travel

In Kobe, Japan, tiny "tunnels" were built for turtles to cross the train tracks safely.

Eugene Bostick of Fort Worth, Texas, built a custom train to take his rescue pups for a ride!

All aboard!

Nitama, a cat, is the stationmaster of the Kishi train station in Japan! Her beloved predecessor, Tama, was even enshrined as a goddess!

The London underground has its own distinct subspecies of mosquito—*Culex pipiens molestus*!

From 1992 to 2012, the waste from New York City rode on a special "poop train" to Colorado for farmers to use on crops!

37

Mo's Bows!

Fourteen-year-old Moziah Bridges started his own bow tie company, Mo's Bows! Moziah has even given President Obama a custom Obama Blue bow tie, and he also served as an ESPN® fashion correspondent at the 2015 NBA® Draft, where a top draft pick wore his bow tie!

Ripley's Asks...

Moziah tied up the loose ends we had about the bow tie biz!

. . . .

Q: How do you balance running a business with your schoolwork?

A: Well, I'm homeschooled, so I usually just do schoolwork at the beginning of the day, and my company work at the end of the day.

Q: Who would you most love to give a bow tie to?

A: I would love to give my ties to Kanye West—he's someone in both the fashion world and music world.

Q: What advice would you give young people dreaming of creating their own business?

A: Invest in yourself, and really take time to think about what you want to achieve in life—and make sure it makes you smile at the end of the day.

crafty

A group of artists called Taxi Fabric is transforming taxis in Mumbai, India, into works of art. Everything from the doors to the steering wheel is covered in colorful designs!

Cabs

Art on the GO!

The night before an Indian bride gets married, the palms of her hands and feet are often painted with amazing henna patterns. Henna has been used to color skin and hair for over 5,000 years!

Design your own henna patterns on this hand.

3 Once the henna is applied, it is left to dry for around 20 minutes.

1 Henna comes from the henna plant.

2 The leaves are crushed and made into a paste, which is applied to the skin in a cool design.

4 The top layer then peels off, revealing the beautiful design underneath.

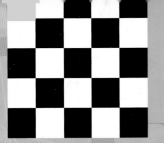

Follow the tire tracks to find out which crafty cab makes it to the Taj Mahal!

1 2 3 4

Kanyakumari Beach

Khari Baoli

Taj Mahal

Hawa Mahal

The Taj Mahal is a white marble mausoleum considered one of the Seven Wonders of the World.

Want to check your answer? Turn to page 137 for the puzzle solution!

Think

Lobster Larry

Sitting in the small town of Kingston SE, Australia, is Larry the lobster—a massive metal crustacean more than 50 feet high!

Mac the Moose

A giant sculpture of a moose welcomes visitors to Moose Jaw, Saskatchewan, Canada. He's more than three stories high!

This page is a-moose-ing!

44

Big!

Don't be so corny!

Field of Corn
In Dublin, Ohio, a former cornfield now houses 109 people-sized ears of concrete corn in one huge, weird art display.

Kelpies
Falkirk in Scotland is home to The Kelpies, the largest equine sculpture in the world at 98 feet high!

45

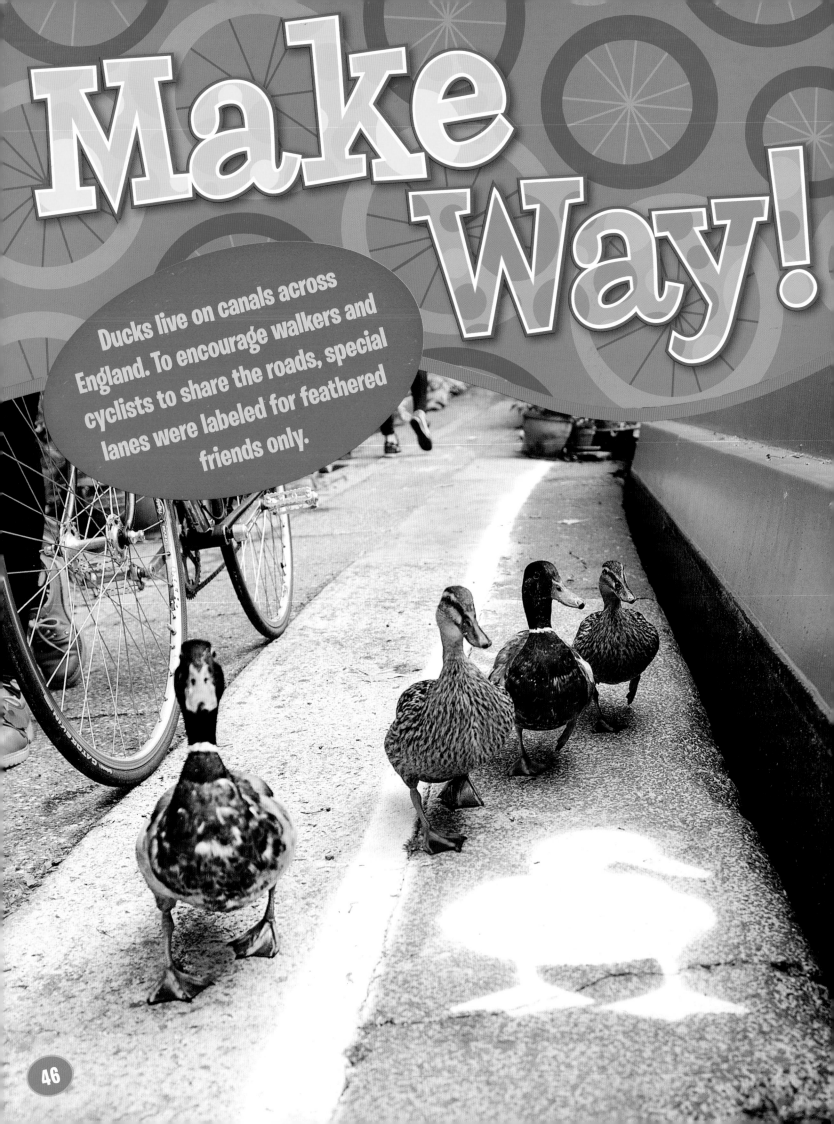

Make Way!

Ducks live on canals across England. To encourage walkers and cyclists to share the roads, special lanes were labeled for feathered friends only.

The 140-foot-tall Eshima Ohashi bridge in Japan offers a thrill ride on the open road. It's known as the "rollercoaster bridge" for its steep incline.

In 1831, Nancy Kerlin Barnett was buried on a hill in Amity, Indiana. Nancy's grandson never let the county build a road over her grave, so her tombstone still stands—in the middle of the road!

MAP FABRICATIONS

"Paper towns" were fake places added to maps by early mapmakers to prevent forgeries of their work.

Until the 18th century, European maps regularly depicted California as an island!

British pilots in World War II carried specially modified maps and a pencils that hid maps and a compass.

Twenty-nine thousand rubber toy animals fell off a ship into the Pacific in 1992. Traveling thousands of miles, they are now used to map ocean currents!

The small "You Are Here" sticker on a map has a name—it's called an ideo locator.

Let's go that way!

In December 2015, a church in Berlin, Germany, hosted a *Star Wars*-themed church service!

FAR FAR AWAY

Scenes on the ice planet Hoth in *The Empire Strikes Back* were really that brutally cold—they were shot on location at the Hardangerjøkulen glacier in Norway during a storm!

Do or do not. There is no try.

There is a species of ocean-dwelling acorn worm named after Yoda—Yoda Purpurata.

The character of Chewbacca was inspired by George Lucas's big, hairy Alaskan malamute dog named Indiana.

Inside the ISS

Here are **five** out-of-this-world **facts** about life on the **International Space Station**, also known as the **ISS!**

Calluses on the ISS astronauts' feet eventually fall off while in space, leaving them soft and smooth like a baby's feet.

On August 10, 2015, NASA astronauts in the ISS ate food that for the first time had been grown in space—red romaine lettuce.

The International Space Station has more livable room than a six-bedroom house!

Astronauts sleep in phone-booth-sized pods!

When astronaut Scott Kelly opened the hatch of the International Space Station, the smell of space reminded him of "burning metal."

HI-SEAS

In Mauna Loa, Hawaii, six volunteer "astronauts" live in a solar-powered dome for a whole year and test space equipment for NASA.

Igor the drone

By living in the Hawaii Space Exploration Analog and Simulation mission (HI–SEAS), they are getting a taste of what life on Mars might be like!

This is an inside view of the HI–SEAS dome. In the main area, the crew eats, works, exercises, and grows plants.

Pets in Space

Is it a bird? Is it a plane? No, it's Daisy, the spectacular flying Chihuahua. Daisy's owner, James Holmdahl of Bend, Oregon, attached his pup to a cluster of helium balloons during the town's Fourth of July Parade!

Peekaboo... I see you!

With the *U-Pet* brand backpack, you can take your kitty out to the ballgame, on a plane, or for a walk!

Welcome to the

The entire Amazon River Basin once flowed in the opposite direction!

Since 2002, scientific expeditions in the Amazon rainforest have revealed 10 new species of bioluminescent mushrooms!

Jungle

The beetle *Agra sasquatch* of the Amazon rainforest is named after Bigfoot because of its large feet!

To help capture its prey, the margay, an Amazonian wildcat, mimics the calls of small tamarin monkeys.

Rainforest Round-Up!

Draw creepy creatures and things you might come across on an Amazonian swim. Don't forget disgusting leeches, snakes, piranhas, and chilling crocodiles!

Rainforests contain more than half of the world's plant and animal species.

Learn more about the amazing rainforests with this fun *crossword puzzle!*

Want to check your answers? Turn to page 137 for the puzzle solution!

ACROSS

2 A chart of the rivers, mountains, and streams of an area

4 A tropical forest

6 The protection of animals, plants, and natural resources

10 A tool for finding direction whose needle points north

11 Having a lot of moisture in the air

DOWN

1 An area with a lot of rain and very tall trees

3 Something that protects an animal by making it hard to see

5 Having a high temperature

7 An animal or plant that is very rare and might die out completely

8 A river in South America

9 Relating to the tropics

61

Wild Africa

After checking the plumbing of hot tubs with missing water, workers at the Etali Safari Lodge in North West Province, South Africa, discovered the culprit was actually a thirsty elephant!

In ancient Egypt, killing a cat was punishable by death!

A beauty contest for sheep is the most popular TV show in Senegal, Africa!

Ewe should pick me!

Baboons were once trained to tend herds of goats in Namibia, protecting them during the day and returning them to their pens at night—sometimes riding the biggest ones!

Madagascar leaf-nosed snakes have a bizarre pointed nose—and nobody knows why.

Flip-Flop Fun!

Ocean Sole® in Nairobi, Kenya, has found a way to recycle flip-flops by creating handmade toys, necklaces, and even life-sized sculptures!

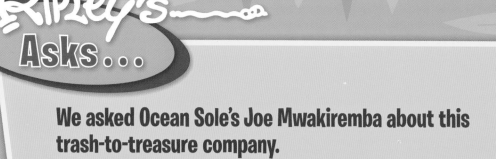

We asked Ocean Sole's Joe Mwakiremba about this trash-to-treasure company.

Q: What was the inspiration to use the flip-flops to make toys?

A: Our founder, Julie Church, observed some children on the island of Kiwayu were making toys out of the flip-flop debris that washed up on the beaches.

Q: How do the flip-flops end up on the beaches?

A: Some are washed away during rainy seasons, and some are carried by ocean currents from as far as Indonesia, creating garbage patches in our oceans.

Wacky Wheels

Starting at the age
of 14, Sudhakar Yadav
of Hyderabad, India,
has built over 200
strange-shaped cars.
He's even created the
Sudha Cars Museum
to house them all!

Cozy Coupe

In November 2013, two British brothers—mechanics John and Geof Bitmead—finished building this adult-sized replica of a Little Tykes® Cozy Coupe. It's actually a modified Daewoo car that can reach speeds of up to 90 mph!

Ripley's Asks...

John and Geof Bitmead explain how they got in gear and created their version of the Cozy Coupe!

....

Q: What kind of reactions do you get when you drive by in the Cozy Coupe?

Geof: Always smiles—even when people are looking miserable, they light up when they see us on the road, which is a fantastic feeling!

Q: Who's the better driver—John or Geof?

John: I've driven around 4,500 miles in it, while Geof and others have driven another 500 miles. So it looks like I am more familiar with the car!

When a young guest at Ireland's Adare Manor Hotel left her stuffed bunny behind, the hotel posted photos of the toy enjoying some five-star treatment at the hotel on Facebook! The pampered bunny was reunited with his owner the next day.

VIP Bunny

Living the good life.

Ralph, a rabbit belonging to Pauline Grant of Sussex, England, weighs 49 pounds!

The Bunny Museum in Pasadena, California, displays over 28,000 rabbit collectibles—along with seven pet bunnies!

Illuminated Igloos

Stay cozy and warm in a heated glass igloo at the Kakslauttanen Arctic Resort in Finland!

Through the igloo's clear ceiling, the colorful aurora borealis, also known as the northern lights, will flash across the night sky as you drift off to sleep.

Do You Wanna Build a Snow Globe?

No two snowflakes are the same.

California

GEORGIA

The largest snowball fight on record took place in Saskatchewan, Canada, with exactly 7,681 snow fighters!

Stuff you need:

- A small, clean glass jar with a lid
- A small plastic toy or figurine—choose one you aren't tempted to play with
- 1-2 tsp. glitter
- Clean water
- Glue
- Paper towel

Here we'll craft, and here we'll play!

1. Glue and stick your plastic toy or figurine to the inside of the jar lid. Place the lid on a paper towel and let the glue dry completely.
2. Next, fill your jar with water and add glitter to the water.
3. Carefully apply glue along the inside rim of the jar's lid. Be careful not to smear any extra glue onto your figurine.
4. Screw the lid on top of the jar and set it aside-right side up-on the paper towel until the glue dries completely.
5. That's it! Shake your jar or tip it upside down to make it snow! (The cold never bothered you anyway!)

Ice Palace Paradise

Every winter when the temperature drops to minus 31°F, you can chill out at the International Ice and Snow Sculpture Festival in Harbin, China—the world's biggest winter festival!

It takes a team of more than 7,000 people to carve the huge buildings and palace sculptures out of ice.

Go on a Polar Expedition

Start at the penguins' home at the bottom of the page and battle through the maze to the fish, avoiding the cracks in the ice. Then try to get back, but this time avoid the seals instead!

TIP!
Use different colors for the journey to the sea and the journey home again.

HOME

Today _____ and I finally _____ to Antarctica! The
person   verb ending in -ed

trip was so _____ that we _____ during dinner
adjective   verb ending in -ed

the first night. Thankfully, we managed to pack enough _____
noun

and _____ for our three-day hike. It was so _____ we
noun   adjective

could not feel our _____ ! We saw some _____ and _____,
noun   animal   animal

and they were so _____ and _____ ! Suddenly, I fell in
adjective   adjective

some cold _____ , so _____ had to help me _____
noun   person   verb

my _____. The best part was _____ the _____
noun   verb ending in -ing   noun

every night by the fire. Before we left, I _____ the
verb ending in -ed

sled dogs and said goodbye to our _____ guide. I hope
adjective

we'll _____ in _____ for another polar expedition!
verb   year

**Ask friends to choose words
to** fill in the blanks in this
story, **but don't let them peek.**
Then, read it out loud!

**Want to check
your answers?**
Turn to page 137
for the puzzle solution!

Got the Munchies?

Fredric Baur invented the Pringles® can. When he passed away in 2008, his ashes were buried in one!

This one goes out to Mars & Murrie!

M&M's® actually stands for "Mars & Murrie's," the last names of the candy's founders.

Ben Cohen, the cofounder of Ben & Jerry's® ice cream, has almost no sense of smell, so when he couldn't taste a recipe, he just kept adding more flavoring!

In 1907, an advertisement for Kellogg's Corn Flakes® offered a **free box of cereal** to any woman who would wink at her grocer.

A 3 Musketeers® originally included **three smaller candy bars: one vanilla, one chocolate, and one strawberry.**

In the US, movie theater popcorn costs more per ounce than filet mignon!

Capybara Cutie

Meet Sweetie—style icon, Internet celebrity, and a capybara, one of the world's largest rodents! This glamorous gal can be spotted window shopping and greeting fans in her hometown of Las Vegas, Nevada.

Emily told us more about her pet capybara!

Q: Sweetie is quite the fashionista. What are some of her favorite outfits?

A: She loves her tutus, dinosaur onesies, animal costumes, and hoodies!

Q: Sweetie is also an animal activist— what's her mission?

A: In some countries, capybaras are hunted, eaten, and used for leather. I hope that through social media, people get to know her and understand these are kind and loving animals who are friends, not food!

I just love pink!

Creature

Europe's kings and queens used to give each other rare and exotic animals as gifts. In the UK, these animals were known as the Royal Menagerie of England, and they lived in the Tower of London for over 600 years!

In 1811, the Hudson Bay Company gave the first grizzly bear ever seen in England to King George III, who named it Martin.

THE TRAITORS' GATE

Collection

That's EMUsing.

In 1828, General Watson gave King George IV a Bengal lion called George as a gift.

Many beasts and fowl called the Tower of London home in 1829, including these crazy critters:

an African porcupine
baboons
a brown coati
a caracal
cheetahs
eagles
elephants
emus
a jaguar
kangaroos
leopards
lions, tigers, and bears

llamas
an ocelot
a paradoxorus
a puma
a secretary bird
hundreds of snakes
a striped hyena
white-headed mongooses
a zebra

Paradoxorus

Food for Thought!

Zoe Fox from Leicestershire, England, spent 300 hours making a life-size tiger out of cake!

Miniature artist Enrique Ramos of Mexico City, Mexico, painted this Aztec scene on a tortilla!

The world's first hedgehog cafe opened in Tokyo, Japan, in 2016!

If you're bored of cereal and milk, maybe try a Rainbow Bagel from The Bagel Store in Brooklyn, New York!

Kid Chef!

With grandparents from Louisiana, the Philippines, Cuba, and Honduras, recipes from 15-year-old professional chef Eliana de Las Casas have an international flair!

Ripley's Asks...

We asked Eliana about her recipe for success!

Q: What was the first recipe you ever created, and how did it turn out?

A: When I was four years old, I created heart-shaped strawberry and cream cheese sandwiches. They were delicious, and I served them at a Valentine's Day party.

Q: What was the funniest thing that's happened while you were cooking?

A: My mom and I roasted chestnuts for the first time, but I didn't research how to roast them and just put them in the oven. Suddenly, it sounded like a popcorn machine exploded. When my mom opened the oven door, chestnuts literally flew out! We didn't know we were supposed to cut slits into the chestnuts to allow the steam to escape. Needless to say, we learned our lesson!

Q: Is there someone famous you'd love to cook for? What would you make for them?

A: I would love to prepare for Ed Sheeran, my favorite musician, a traditional Louisiana meal of jambalaya, gumbo, and shrimp étouffée, with pralines as a sweet treat.

Let's Get Cooking!

An Internet star since she was eight, Eliana's YouTube cooking tutorials led to her own web radio show and three award-winning cookbooks. Try making Eliana's delicious pizza recipe!

TWO-INGREDIENT PIZZA DOUGH

(Serves 2)

Stuff you need:
- 1 cup self-rising flour
- 1 cup Greek yogurt
- olive oil
- baking sheet
- medium-size bowl
- pizza sauce
- cheese
- toppings for pizza

Do it yourself:
1. Preheat oven to 400°F.
2. Using the olive oil, grease a baking sheet.
3. In a medium bowl, combine flour and yogurt. Mix until it forms a ball.
4. Divide the ball in half and place on a flat, floured surface.
5. Roll out the balls to form small, circular pizzas.
6. Place on greased baking sheet.
7. Drizzle a little olive oil on top.
8. Add sauce, cheese, and then toppings for pizza.
9. Bake for 20 minutes. Enjoy!

Look for Your Lunch

Hungry? Find these 15 foods from around the world. Make sure you look up, down, across, and diagonally!

CURRY

FLAN

POUTINE

CREPE

FONDUE

RAMEN

DUMPLING

KEBAB

SUSHI

FAJITA

KIMCHI

TACO

FETA

PIZZA

WASABI

```
C U R R Y L Z K L Q U I P Z A
R E D D A H O I Z A E K O H I
E L D T A C M M W M U W U W L
P C U M H B H S D G M I T I X
E Q E A A W O H S U S H I B M
T Z U B W S P I A S N O N A A
J U E R O N S P A A R K E S B
T K Q C D U M P L I N G A A R
F O A D T Z O F A A B W I W O
M T K R A M E N E A T Q N E R
L A Z Z C F T T S E U D N O F
Q C A P B F K A P W U A S N P
N W A O R E W C F K J J S U Z
P A U O N T P I Z Z A P I A S
F A J I T A C S X A B T A C W
```

Peas look carefully!

Want to check your answers? Turn to page 137 for the puzzle solution!

Forktress

If you have a hero-sized appetite, then grab a bite at the DC Comics® Super Heroes Café in Singapore!

the STARTERS

SOUP OF THE DAY
DAILY PLANET $9.9

SP 1. SUPERMAN'S SOUP
SIGNATURE CHICKEN SAUSAGE
GUMBO WITH PARMESAN LAVOSH $11.9

SL 2. GREEN LANTERN V... CAESAR SALAD
CRISP ROMAINE LETTUCE, SHAVE...
PARMESAN, BLACK OLIVES, CAES...
DRESSING AND GARLIC TOAST

SL 1. CLARK & DIANA'S ANTI-COBB SALAD
MESCLUN SALAD WITH AVOCADO, APPLE, STRAWBERRY,
MANGO, HONEYDEW AND ORANGE SEGMENT TOSSED WITH
HONEY CITRUS YOGURT DRESSING $19.9

POWER UP! ADDITIONAL TOP...
SMOKED SALMON
GRILLED CHICKEN MEAT

# of Solitude

Fans can choose their favorite DC character-inspired food from a colorful comic book menu and enjoy their meal while sitting at themed tables, surrounded by incredible collectibles.

Kara Zor-El

WEIGHT: 135lbs EYES: Blue HAIR: Blonde

Adventurer BASE: Metropolis

RS / ABILITIES: Under the Sun's solar radiation, Supergirl's kryptonian
bs energy and can fly, has superstrength, superspeed, invulnerability,
nd a range of vision including emitting X-rays and heat.

Stanley Lau

REAL NAME: BARTHOLOMEW "BARRY" ALLEN
HEIGHT 5ft 11in WEIGHT: 179lbs EYES Blue HAIR Blonde
OCCUPATION Police chemist BASE: Central City
SPECIAL POWERS / ABILITIES Could run at near lightspeed could
vibrate or phase into other dimensions.

ILLUSTRATION BY: Stanley Lau

12

Monumental Madness

The Great Wall of China was built with earth, stones, and RICE!

It took over 1,000 elephants to carry the materials used to build the Taj Mahal.

Nailed it.

It is illegal to take a photograph of the Eiffel Tower at night.

But first, let me take a selfie!

Clap your hands in front of Chichen Itza's El Castillo pyramid, and the echo will sound like a chirping bird.

The Statue of Liberty has a 4½ ft. long nose and an 8 ft. long index finger!

Monumental Mazes

PYRAMID SCHEME

Make it out of the maze, but don't get trapped in the treasure rooms!

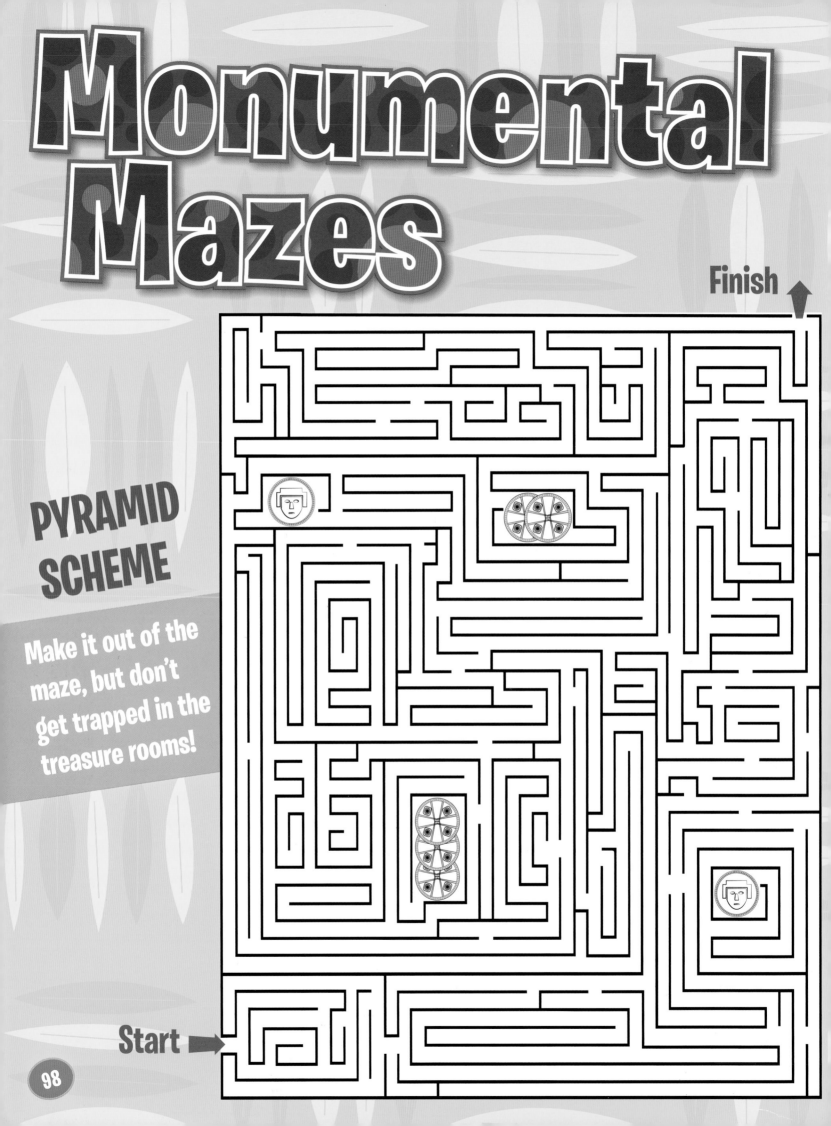

Start ▶

STONEHENGE REVENGE

Start

Find your way through the maze to get to Stonehenge!

The 40-ton stones used to build Stonehenge were moved and positioned more than 20 miles without the benefit of the wheel!

Want to check your answers? Turn to page 138 for the puzzle solutions!

Cinderella Church

This glittering fairy tale-style glass slipper in Taiwan is actually a church for "happily ever after" weddings! It's made up of 320 tinted glass panels, stands over five stories tall, and took only two months to build!

The World Bathtubbing Championships are a series of races where competitors kayak in a bathtub!

MOVE IT!

Every year the Ascot Races in the UK have a Lamb National, where a herd of sheep fence jump, each one with a little teddy bear jockey.

Switzerland's Mount Niesen is home to the world's longest single staircase race, known as Niesenlauf. Reaching the top is equal to climbing the Empire State Building more than seven times!

Set Sail!

Although there are over 7,000 islands, only about 2 percent of the Caribbean is inhabited!

KO-KEE, KO-KEE.

The male coqui frog of Puerto Rico is less than 2 inches long, but its croak is as loud as a passing jet!

The pink sand found on the beaches of Harbour Island in the Bahamas gets its color from millions of microscopic animals with bright pink and red shells.

ACTUAL SIZE

Barbados is home to the world's smallest snake. It's just 4 inches long and as wide as a spaghetti noodle!

Some people love to perform tricks on their bikes, but Cirque Mechanics takes it to a whole new level! This "circus on wheels" performs on trampolines, trapezes, high wires, and more—all while riding amazing bicycle-based machines.

Cirque Mechanics

Ripley's Asks...

Director Chris Lashua brings us up to speed on Cirque Mechanics!

Q: What inspired the idea to form a circus troupe on bicycles?

A: I started doing tricks on a BMX® bicycle when I was 12 years old, and haven't stopped.

Q: Do you build the contraptions and machines the troupe uses?

A: Yes, I do. Designing, cutting, prepping the materials at the fabrication shop, painting, and then watching an artist use it is fantastic.

Q: What kind of precautions do you take to stay safe on your bikes?

A: We use crash mats and spotters, and we take it slow to make sure our routines are consistent and reliable. Safety always comes first!

107

Amusement Park Word Search

Can you find all 15 things hidden in this puzzle? Make sure to look up, down, backward, across, and diagonally!

COTTON CANDY

WATER RIDE

POPCORN

FUNNEL CAKE

HOT DOGS

CAROUSEL

FERRIS WHEEL

MUSIC

GAMES

BUMPER CAR

PRIZES

PARADE

FIREWORKS

TICKETS

CANDY

M	J	S	F	B	L	Z	M	L	Q	U	F	G	I	G
U	E	T	U	U	H	A	I	Z	E	D	A	R	A	P
S	L	E	N	M	F	P	N	S	E	T	T	O	O	H
I	C	K	N	P	R	I	Z	E	S	M	R	P	I	W
E	A	C	E	E	P	O	P	C	O	Y	C	B	A	A
N	N	I	L	R	R	S	W	H	D	O	O	T	H	N
N	D	T	C	C	N	S	P	N	R	R	E	I	O	B
U	T	Q	A	A	B	T	A	N	I	R	N	C	T	R
F	O	X	K	R	Z	C	L	A	R	H	I	I	D	O
M	U	S	E	C	N	N	N	I	D	S	G	N	O	R
L	G	L	Y	O	S	O	D	T	U	O	A	D	G	G
Q	I	P	T	O	D	E	U	M	W	U	M	E	S	P
N	E	T	F	E	R	R	I	S	W	H	E	E	L	Z
N	O	N	N	E	L	C	A	R	O	U	S	E	L	N
C	A	N	D	I	B	S	K	R	O	W	E	R	I	F

Want to check
your answers?
Turn to page 138
for the puzzle solution!

Zany Zoos

WHO likes to read?

An Eagle Owl named Yoda keeps pesky seagulls away from the University of Bath campus in England. In appreciation, the university gave Yoda his very own library card!

Before flying from Australia to the Singapore Zoo, one lucky koala enjoyed hot towels and eucalyptus leaves in a first-class photo session with Qantas airlines.

This is the life.

When tourists in India's Bandipur National Park stopped to snap photos of an elephant and her calf, the hungry mama suddenly reached into their car and scarfed down a handbag, including some gold jewelry!

Flushed

With Joy

In 2014, a museum in Tokyo, Japan, hosted an exhibit where people learned about toilets, sewage, and health—it featured singing toilets, a "poop lady" mascot, and a giant toilet slide!

Don't forget to flush!

The Great Stalacpipe Organ uses Virginia's Luray Caverns to produce music—softly striking the cave's stalactites to produce sound!

Offbeat

In Zadar, Croatia, architect Nikola Bašić created the Sea Organ, a set of 35 organ pipes that make beautiful music as waves lap at the coastline.

Deep in Estonia's Võru County forest, students installed three giant wooden megaphones for visitors to sit inside and listen to the forest.

Fun Sized

Just 32 inches tall, 15-year-old Raman Raikvar is half the size of most kids his age, and he plans to become the world's tiniest stand-up comedian!

Rapid Reader

Eleven-year-old Faith Jackson of Cheshire, England, read 942 books in 2014—and completed an incredible 1,151 books in 2015! Impressed, author Holly Webb dedicated her book *The Forgotten Puppy* to Faith, and Lucy Coats dedicated *Beasts of Olympus: The Steeds of the Gods.*

BEASTS OF OLYMPUS
STEEDS OF THE GODS

Illustrated by
DAVID ROBERTS

LUCY COATS

Ripley's Asks...

We asked Faith to tell us the story behind all the stories she's read.

Q: What inspired you to read so many books in a year?

A: My mum inspired me to start reading, and then I decided I wanted to read as many as humanly possible!

Q: Have you set a goal for this coming year?

A: I've decided that it's crazy to set another "number goal," so instead, I'm aiming to write a short review of every book I read in 2016!

Painted

In Zalipie, a secluded village in southeastern Poland, the houses bloom with color! Following a centuries-old tradition, Zalipie women paint their homes in bright floral patterns.

Village

Take turns with your friends and choose words to fill in the blanks...

WACKY WALKABOUT

...the sillier, the better!

_____ and I just _____ our Australian walkabout, and
   Person   **verb ending in -ed**

it was _____! We started in the morning, _____ in the
     adjective   **verb ending in -ing**

bush with our guides. Right away we saw _____ kangaroos
                                            adjective

_____ around and _____ koalas in the trees.
verb ending in -ing   **adjective**

We even saw roaming emus. Those are _____! At times
                                        adjective

we heard _____ cockatoos in the _____ and saw monitor
        adjective   **noun**

lizards _____ under rocks and boulders. I thought we
      verb ending in -ing

would see _____, but we were not so lucky. At night we heard
        noun

some possums as they _____ for _____, and we saw fruit
               verb ending in -ed   **noun**

bats that looked like flying foxes. Finally, I got _____ by
                                    verb ending in -ed

a wolf spider! Can you believe it? The _____ hurt only a little,
                                noun

but it was super itchy! This trip was so _____, and I can't
                                     adjective

wait to do it again!

Ripley's— Strange Mail

Bee Hive

Wicker Jar of Almonds

Avocado

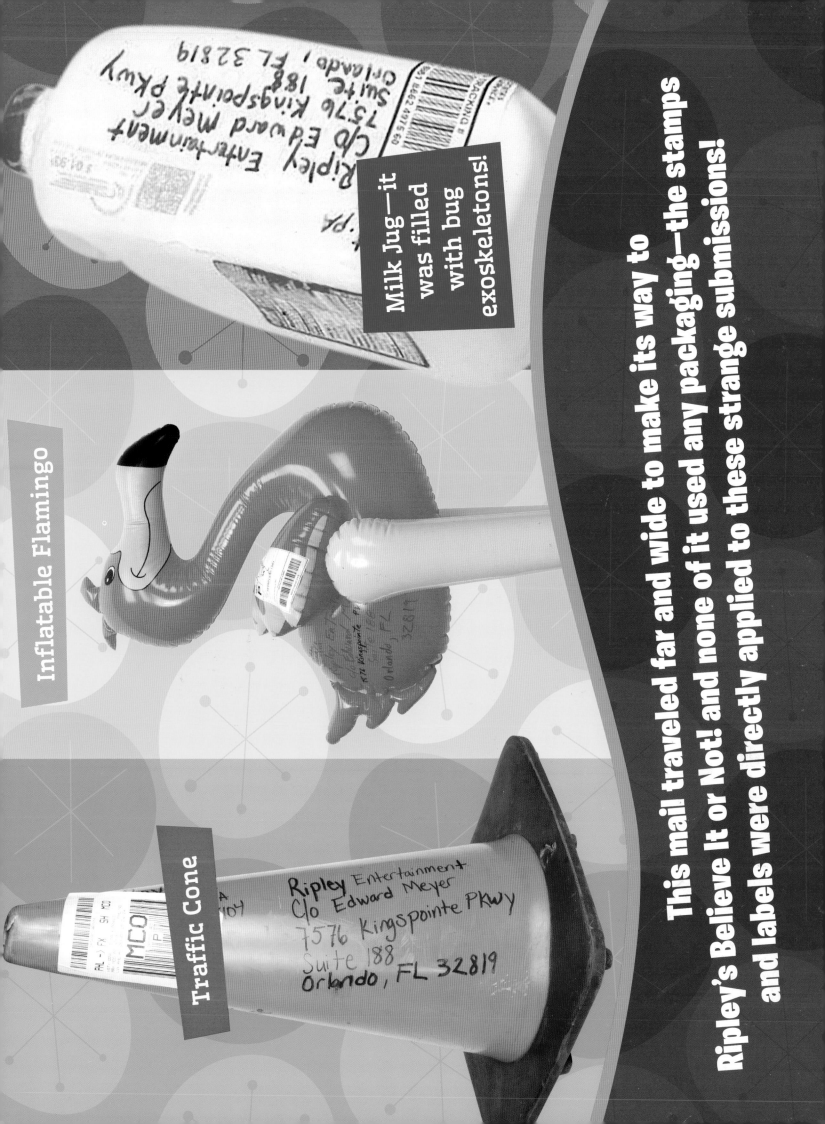

Milk Jug—it was filled with bug exoskeletons!

Inflatable Flamingo

Traffic Cone

Ripley Entertainment
C/o Edward Meyer
7576 Kingspointe PKWY
Suite 188
Orlando, FL 32819

This mail traveled far and wide to make its way to Ripley's Believe It or Not! and none of it used any packaging—the stamps and labels were directly applied to these strange submissions!

CRAZY COUNTRIES

Russians have no word for blue—Russian has separate phrases for "light blue" and "dark blue," but none for "blue."

Two churches on the Greek island of Chios celebrate Easter by firing thousands of rockets at each other.

Every year, tourists throw over $1,000,000 in coins into the Trevi Fountain in Rome!

In Greece, some olive trees planted in the thirteenth century are still producing olives!

Flooded village Curon Venosta in Italy sits underwater—but its bell tower still juts above the water's surface!

Feathers in Flight

The wild budgerigar of Australia swarm in the thousands—even millions— when in search of food and water!

Madison, Wisconsin's official bird is the plastic pink flamingo!

Green parakeets nest in the crater of the active Massaya Volcano in Nicaragua!

In February 2016, Lynn Campbell of Aberdeenshire, Scotland, photographed a sparrow in her garden with a very rare, abnormally large beak!

129

Bon Voyage!

Fill in the blanks with the correct mode of transportation. Then order the numbered letters to reveal the secret message!

1 This hovers and watches traffic.

___ ___ ___ ___ ___ ___ ___
                              1   10   7

2 Glide along the tracks in this. Choo choo!

___ ___ ___ ___ ___
11   5   4

3 Fly in the sky on this.

___ ___ ___ ___ ___ ___
3   12   14   9

4 Hold on tight while the dogs pull you along.

___ ___ ___ ___
   6   8

5 Pedal and balance on this. Once you know how, you never forget.

___ ___ ___ ___ ___
  13   2

UNSCRAMBLE THE SECRET MESSAGE

___ ___ ___ ___ ___ ___ ___ ___ ___ ___ ___ ___ ___ ___ !
1 2 3 4   5   6   7 8 9 10   11 12 13 14

Help the lost husky find his way to the dog sled!

Want to check your answers? Turn to pages 138 for the puzzle solutions!

In 2001 Frenchman Marco Siffredi descended from the summit of Mount Everest on a snowboard!

Mount Everest's Nepali name, Sagarmatha, means "head of the sky"!

Australian artist Edgy has exhibited his paintings at Mount Everest base camp at 17,598 feet!

Everest

The Himalayan jumping spider lives at 22,000 feet up on Mount Everest and preys on insects carried up on the wind. It can leap 30 times its own length!

Here are some of the places we've visited—ODD AROUND THE WORLD! Use this handy guide for saying "Hello" and "Goodbye"!

World

Olá

Здравствуйте

Hola

Ciao

Bonjour

Halló

您好

Salut

こんにちは

Guten Tag

안녕하세요

Travelers

Agur

नमस्कार

مع السلام

Slán

Arrivederci

Au revoir

안녕히 가세요

Adiós

Tchau

再见

135

Worldwide Whirly Word, pages 8-9

```
P J R F Q L Z B L Q U F G I A
J E D D A H O I Z A E K J H I
E L D T M G M N W M U W K S L
A C U M H A N O D G M O T I X
S Q E A L W E X F O R U B O A
T Z U D W S W S A I N O E H N
J U M R K N Y P A Q R K I N B
T T Q I D B O C G I N N J D R
F O X D E Z R L A A H W I R O
M T K R T N K N E D T Q N E R
L G L V S F T T Z B V H G V K
Q I P P O D K U P W U I E N P
N E M O R M W N F K J J Q N Z
T O R O N T O I I P D B P I P S
P A R I S A C S X A B A F A D
```

Animal Round-Up, page 19

FROG

Animal Round-Up, page 18

A-MAZE-ING Airlines, page 23

136

Your Odd Adventure, page 30

Four-letter word answers

aunt	neat
dare	need
dart	rate
date	rent
deer	tear
duet	tree
even	true
ever	vent

Five-letter word answers

averted	tender
deter	trade
eater	tundra
enter	under
nature	unread
never	veteran
raven	
tavern	

Art on the GO!, page 43

Go on a Polar Expedition, page 78

The red line shows their journey to eat.

The blue line shows their journey back home.

Look for your Lunch, page 93

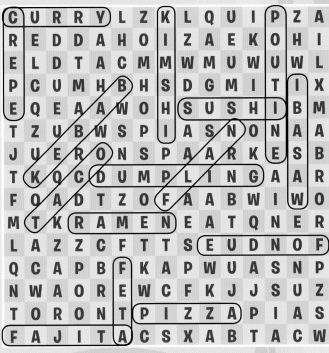

Rainforest Round-Up, page 61

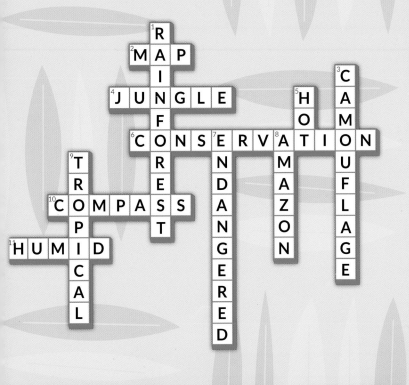

PYRAMID SCHEME

STONEHENGE REVENGE

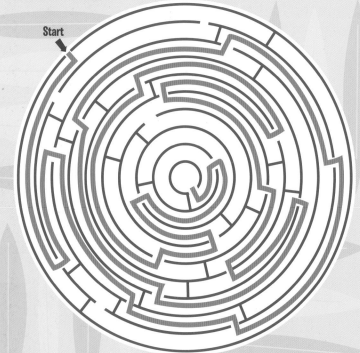

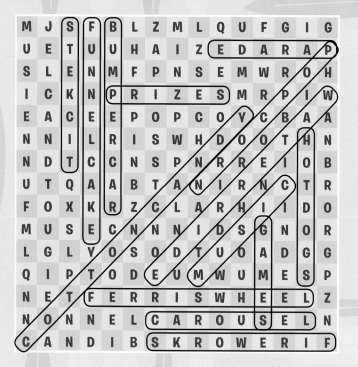

Bon Voyage!, pages 130–131

H E L I C O P T E R
1   10   7

T R A I N
11 5   4

A I R P L A N E
3   12 14   9

D O G S L E D
6   8

B I C Y C L E
13   2

UNSCRABBLE THE SECRET MESSAGE

P L A N   A   G R E A T   T R I P !
1 2 3 4   5   6 7 8 9 10   11 12 13 14